Fish On! Shore: Gulf Shores/Orange Beach

Fish On!
Shore

Gulf Shores/Orange Beach

By Matthew C. Willett

As the truck door closed, I opened my eyes. Dawn was creeping up, and it'd been a long night of floundering. I was beat, and we hadn't caught much.

He spoke without turning, face lit dim by the dashboard panel light as he turned the key in the ignition.

"Well, at least we didn't get skunked."

I'll never forget the way he smiled.

Ray Heidelberg
1925-2007

Granddaddy

Acknowlegements:

I owe a special debt of gratitude to the fishing guides cited in this book. Without their generosity and willingness to share their knowlege, this book would have never happened. Further special mention goes to Captain Don Holloway, without whom I might have never caught that cover fish. I can't express my gratitude for Todd Robinson, who, with his wife Andi and sons Tyler and Tucker, posed for the cover (not to mention for everything he teaches me on Sunday mornings). All my love and appreciation is due to my Oma, Loretta Heidelberg, who's always supported me (and fed me!), my mother, Connie Teague, who was my first grammar teacher, and all those editors and teachers at Auburn who taught me how to do this. We should all thank Jenny James, who said, "Why don't you tell some Ray stories?" Her idea pulled this book together.

Finally, to everyone I've fished with over the years, and to my church family at Silverhill First Baptist and all my friends and family: Thank you all. You mean the world to me.

About this book:

This book has everything you need to know to catch fish right from the shore. Tasty fish. Tough sport fish. Fish kids can land and fish everyone on the beach will admire.

It's not aimed at making you a tournament-winning angler, or teaching old salts new tricks. Whether you've fished saltwater in the past or freshwater your whole life or never fished at all, this book lays it out. The tackle, the tactics and the tools you'll need to go from laying on the beach to learning the lay of the beach, from just laying around to laying fish, good fish, out on the beach: it's all right here.

This book is full of local knowledge anyone can use to catch saltwater fish right from the shore here in Gulf Shores and Orange Beach. It features the know-how of an all-star cast of veteran inshore and near-shore fishing guides from this coast, charter boat captains with nearly a hundred years of combined time on the water who know how to catch anything and everything that swims. It's got the who, what, where, when and how you want to know from the locals who know it best.

You don't have to buy this book to catch fish from the shore. Fishing is unpredictable, and every dog has his day, and I truly hope you'll have great luck even if you don't use the information in this book.

But if you don't buy this book and end up with sunburnt shoulders, exhausted from fighting the waves and jellyfish-stung from the neck down with nothing to show for it but a ladyfish you'll end up throwing back anyway, well — don't blame me.

Now let's catch some fish!

Table of Contents

Introduction

That's me in the picture above. The little one. The big one is my Granddaddy, and that picture was taken in about 1977 or so. I don't recall who took it, but I know it was on the banks of the Intercoastal Canal in Gulf Shores. All these years later the details are fuzzy, but I'll never forget that day. It was my first fishing trip.

I remember the canal bank looking like an impossibly high cliff beneath me, and I remember Granddaddy holding on to my belt to catch me if I slipped. I remember holding that rod in my hands and wishing a fish would bite. I don't remember if we caught fish or not, though I know Granddaddy almost never got skunked when he went fishing. That's just the way he was.

I don't know if Ray's best friend Johnny Oblak was there that day, though he was most every other time we went fishing. I do clearly recall Granddaddy talking to some other fishermen that day, and though I guess I wasn't old enough to pay much attention to what they said, I know he called them "sir" because he always did, no matter who it was. Ray Heidelberg loved to talk to people. I think that's something he had in common with most anglers, not to mention most of the folks on our beach.

Granddaddy took me fishing throughout my childhood: white trout fishing over the oyster shells on Weeks Bay in the boat he built when I was about 12, the boat that's my boat now, floundering in that boat when I got old enough to stay out all night on the water in Orange Beach and then, later, off a little pier on Cotton Bayou when he got to where he didn't like the trouble of putting the boat in the water anymore.

Those days and nights are seared into my memory: images of the moonlight on the water and the way coffee tastes with the scent of salt in your nose.

Those days and nights are seared into my memory: images of the moonlight on the water and the way coffee tastes with the scent of salt in your nose. Like most people, I guess, I didn't listen to my Granddaddy near enough, and I didn't learn a sixteenth of what he knew about fishing. I learned about calling people sir, though, no matter who they are, and I learned about quitting when you've got enough for the freezer. I learned about how good it was to take a break from what you're doing and have someone talk to you like you're sensible, grown up. I learned about the value of being able to take an afternoon or a night for yourself, of being outside doing something worthwhile, about using the time and the resources God gives us wisely.

My hope is that this book can give you a chance to learn some of that while you learn how to enjoy some of the fishing we do down here. If you don't take anything else from this book, remember this: it only takes one breath when you're fishing to make it a great day, one breath when you close your eyes and really breathe it, really feel it, really experience it in a way that sears it into your memory.

I honestly don't remember the last time Granddaddy and I went fishing, the last time we were alone on the water together, quiet, just being there, peaceful and catching fish. In a way, I guess, I don't remember it because it hasn't happened yet. See, Granddaddy's still there every time I fish, and I believe he always will be. He's there with me every time I get on the water, every time I wet a line, every time I taste the salt in the air. I'm a little older now, and I don't fit into that windbreaker anymore, but he's still there, still holding on to my belt.

As my Granddaddy would say when he finished talking to someone about fishing, "Aw'right den, sir. Good luck."

I. Tackle & Equipment

S witch rods with me. That's the only thing it could be. Switch rods with me."

It was one of those perfect days on the water: not too hot, clear and calm and not another boat on the oyster-shell beds on Weeks Bay. The ice chest was filling up with white trout. The only drawback was they were all coming off Granddaddy's hooks. Granddaddy was fishing two rods like he always did, and he'd cast them out to the same spot I did, but his lines always hooked up, usually with both hooks. Mine didn't. I'd

Spinning reels are often called open–faced reels, and are characterized by their exposed spool and the bale, a steel line guide that's pinned back to allow line to feed off the spool during casting.

spent the last hour on the front of the boat cutting bait and putting fresh ones on his hooks and watching my baits get soggy and my lines hang slack.

Now, Granddaddy was sitting at the front of the boat unhooking his own fish and putting them in the ice chest himself, and I'd already traded for the rear seat in a failed attempt to even the odds.

"You'd better cut up another croaker," he'd said. "I think I got a double again." Sure enough, when he finished reeling in his line, two long white trout were hooked at it's end just above the lead weight. That's when I demanded we switch rods. It was all I could think of that could be keeping him catching fish and me cutting bait.

"Maybe that's it," he said with a grin. "Yeah, that's got to be it. It's the rod you're using."

Granddaddy laughed and threw out my old soggy bait.

A minute later he had another double.

Equipment Checklist
Look on page 90 for a detailed and complete buyer's guide of tackle and equipment needs.

Rods & Reels

If you're aiming to fish from the shore, you'll need the right rod, and if you're shopping for the perfect fishing stick, you're bound to end up scratching your head before it's all over.

For most of the shore fishing you'll encounter, whether it's at a seawall or a jetty or on the surf in front of a condo, a 7-foot spinning rod outfit will deliver the most bang for the buck.

Most spinning rods locate the drag control at the front of the spool.

Putting together the right rig, however, can be trickier than you might think.

The first thing you need to know is that an el-cheapo 6-foot spinning combo is a bigger waste of money in this water than a cane pole.

"If you're in town for a week, and you're just looking for a throw-away rod, it may work fine for you," A-Team Fishing's Captain Bobby Abruscato said. "It's better, though, to get a good reel than it is to get a reel that will last for a week that you'll start having problems with. If you can, invest some money in a good set-up. It's possible to get lucky and use a lower-quality set-up and catch a little whiting or something like that, but if you hook up with a redfish or a small shark, a decent bluefish or a mackerel or even, possibly, a ladyfish, it can destroy almost any kind of small reel."

The problem with a 6-foot light-action rod is its lack of "backbone," Captain DeJuan Tedder of Gulf Adventures Charters said. On his boat, the No Excuses, Tedder likes to outfit people with a rod that can handle a wide variety of saltwater fish. "I use 7-foot medium-action rods. They're flexible enough for small fish, but a medium-action rod gives you a little backbone for some of the bigger fish you might encounter."

Rod action can be a personal choice when you're making your selection in the tackle store, but area guides are in agreement that a 7-foot medium-action rod has the perfect blend of "backbone" and the length needed for making long casts. A shorter rod just won't put your bait where the fish are.

"Unless you're planning to throw it away, get a 7-foot medium-light action rod," Baby Therapy Captain Jeff

Rods by the numbers: Fishing rods are rated according to length (in feet and inches) and action, or stiffness. The heavier an action, the stiffer a rod is. Stiffer rods put more pressure on a fish, but lighter-action rods offer more sensitivity. Finally, most rod manufacturers indicate on the rod what line strength (in pounds) and lure weight the rod is designed to use.

Chambliss said. "Most people come down and use tackle that's too heavy ... (That can) put too much pressure on a fish when you don't need it and rip the hook out of its mouth."

If you expect to hook into bigger fish like a speckled (or spotted sea) trout, though, you might consider a medium-heavy rod, though it's good to find one with a fast tip. "I like a 7-foot rod in medium action or a medium-heavy action, but with a fast tip," Spectacklelure's Captain Yano Serra said. "I want that fast tip so I can feel the bite and so I can get enough backbone to set the hook in him."

You'll usually find a rod's vital statistics, its length and action, printed just in front of the grip.

A cheap combo may be tempting, and if you're on a budget it may seem the best choice, but guides say your rod and reel is the most important part of catching fish. Using the right equipment is a key to success, and a rod doesn't have to break your budget. "You need a 7-foot spinning rod," veteran guide Don Holloway said. "It doesn't have to be graphite, and you can get one for $20 or $25."

Rod Materials
Fishing rods can be made of graphite, carbon fibers, fiberglass or composites of these or other materials.

Reels

You could find some savings in your rod selection, but reel choice, the experts say, is no

20

Pro-tip
Always rinse your reel off with fresh water after you finish fishing for the day. Salts from salt water can corrode even the best reels, so rinsing them off will keep your reel working longer.

place to skimp. Salt water can be tough on a line retrieval machine, and, beyond durability, you'll want a reel that has enough line capacity and a good drag system, a way for fish to take line instead of breaking the line when they set off on a run.

The best combination of casting characteristics, toughness and fish-fighting power, guides say, is a spinning reel. "They're easier to clean up after you use them and more likely to withstand the vacation and be able to be used again," Tedder said. Bay Ranger Captain Frank Ford praises the spinning reel as user-friendly and effective.

Spincasters, left, are different than spinning reels, right, because they don't have an open face.

"A spinning outfit is something anyone can cast with just a few minutes of practice. Anyone can use one, and they'll hold a good-sized fish as long as you have the drag set properly," he said. In his next breath, however, he cautioned against using a spinning reel with too little line capacity. "You could hook a 150-pound tarpon on the next cast, and if you do, and your drag is set too light, he'll spool you. You don't want to use tackle that's too light, or he'll be gone."

Most guides in the area prefer to load spinning reels with 12- to 15-pound-test line. Don't be fooled into thinking that's too light for big fish. "I've caught up to 145-pound fish on 15-pound test," Ford said. The key consideration in choosing a lighter line is that it can cast greater distances.

"What a lot of people don't understand is that a bigger line is heavier to cast. They're out there wading in chest-deep water and throwing their bait just 40 feet in front of them," Holloway said. "If you've got lighter line you can throw it much farther and keep your feet dry," he laughed. Chambliss echoed his sentiments.

Spinning reels operate by allowing line to be pulled unobstructed off the spool, so the first guide on a rod designed for a spinning reel will be larger to accomodate the line's wide motion.

"You need a lighter line. You can cast it farther and have more line if a fish makes a run," he said. Using a thin but strong braided line is a good choice, he added. "You're not likely to get spooled. Most of the time you don't need that much, but if you go to the pier and hook a bonita or a small King Mackerel you'll need, at a bare minimum, 150 yards of line."

Note the fact that Chambliss calls 150 yards a "bare minimum." Abruscato said shore-fishing presents issues a boat fishermen can work around with mobility. "Make sure it holds enough line," Abruscato said. "Put 12- to 15-pound line on it, and make sure it has enough capacity to handle a decent amount of line, about 300 yards of 12-pound test. If it happens that you hook something of a fairly decent size, you're

Line Capacity
A quality reel will save you money in the long run. Make sure to note whether it has enough line capacity before you buy. Reels usually are marked to indicate their capacity for a variety of line sizes.
Example:
12/280
15/250
20/200

not able to chase it if you're on shore. Make sure you have enough capacity to handle it."

"With spinning outfits, I wouldn't dwell on gear ratio. They're pretty standardized. With spinning reels the most important thing is quality."

To summarize, start with a 7-foot spinning rod (don't buy a rod designed for a bait-caster — there IS a difference! Look for a larger line guide close to the reel seat, the quick give-away that the rod's designed for a spinning reel.), and mate it with a durable spinning reel that will hold enough line. Most guides say it's best not to get caught up worrying about retrieve ratios, the number of turns the spool makes per turn of the handle (4.1:1 or 5.9:1, etc.), the number of bearings in a reel or other technical considerations.

"With spinning outfits, I wouldn't dwell on gear ratio. They're pretty standardized," Abruscato said. "With spinning reels, the most important thing is quality. Get one with a good drag system that will hold up to salt-water use."

Remember that your rod, reel and line form an integrated system for landing fish — all the parts have to fit together. Don't be put off if manufacturers use different language to indicate what kind of rods, reels and lines go together well. "Usually the rod will tell you. Even if it doesn't say 'medium-heavy,' it'll give you a line rating, for example, 12- to 15-lb. test. You've got to match the line up with the rod," Abruscato said.

Fishin FAQ:
Drag
What's a drag? A drag system is a mechanism built into a reel that allows a fish to 'drag' line off, tiring itself and keeping your line from breaking.

Line

What type of line, monofilament, fluorocarbon or braided, is up to you and how much money you're willing to invest. Each has its plusses and minuses.

Monofilament and fluorocarbon lines can develop line memory over time and create loops in the line that will affect casting distance or cause tangles. Mono-filament line is also

Make sure to buy enough line to spool your reel with one continuous length of line; line can't be spliced together and hold up against a fighting fish.

susceptible to stretching and abrasion. Braided line has a far smaller diameter than monofilament line of the same strength rating, or pound-test rating, making it easier to cast for distance, but, compared to monofilament line, it's expensive and can be difficult to use.

Tackle shops are great sources for information. If you have any questions about line benefits or drawbacks, ask! Choosing the right line will put you on the way to catching great fish.

Line memory
Monofilament and fluorocarbon lines, over time, develop line memory, causing the line to stay in coils even when cast. It's better to use fresh line if you want to avoid time-consuming tangles.

Pier fishing

Before closing the section on rods and reels, it's important to note that pier fishing presents unique challenges that require unique equipment.

If you're planning on fishing exclusively from the Gulf State Park Pier, you'll need a stouter rod since you stand a greater chance of hooking into stouter fish like King Mackerel or shark.

"If you're stepping up to King Mackerel or Jack Cravalle (pronounced "krah-val"), fishing a big live bait off the end of the pier, then you'll want a medium-action 7-and-a-half- or 8-foot medium-action rod and a reel that'll hold 25- or 30-pound test line," Captain Chambliss said.

If pier fishing's your primary interest, check with a local bait shop, call or visit the Gulf State Park Pier to get plenty of information about all the specialized tackle and equipment you'll need.

Few things in life will look better than the ocean growing to meet you as you emerge onto the beach for a session fishing from the shore.

Fish On! Shore: Gulf Shores/Orange Beach

II. Terminal Tackle

We'll see," Granddaddy said as he reached into his spare tackle box.

It was overcast that day, and for the life of me I can't recall where we were or what we were fishing for, but I know it was on his old 14-foot fiberglass V-hull, and I remember the waves rocking us enough to stir my 8-year-old fears. The water had risen almost to white-caps, and we'd been thinking about turning in for the day. At that moment, though, going home

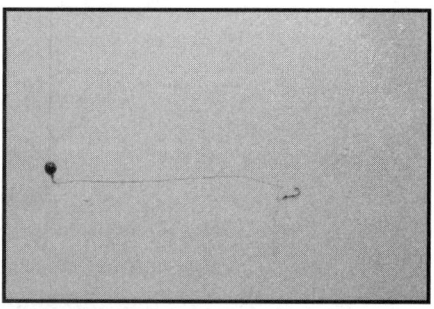

The business end of your rig is one of the most important things to consider when you're aiming at catching supper.

wasn't an option for me or for Granddaddy. I'd just dropped my first rod-and-reel combo over the side, and neither one of us wanted to leave it behind.

Granddaddy'd put it together for me, an old Zebco 33 and a short, light-green rod. He'd taught me how to press the button and hold it and cast, and I'd spent at least a jillion hours, I reckon, before I'd managed to get the rubber practice weight on its line over the power line that led through the air from the garage to the barn. By now, I could switch that brown-plastic pistol-grip from my right hand to my left before the bait sunk two feet into the water and be ready to set the hook and start reeling if a fish hit, but I'd just watched it slip out of my hand and disappear into the drink.

Granddaddy's tackle box looked, to me, like a museum of fishing. It was filled with giant balsa-wood bass plugs and half-melted plastic grubs and tangles of rusty hooks he'd never let me touch. Now he pulled out the biggest treble hook he had, one I'd never seen him use, and tied this monstrosity to the end of his line behind one of the cast-net weights he'd forged before I was born.

A treble hook has three barbed, fish-catching points.

"We'll see," he said again, again casting it a few feet out from the side of the boat and again coming up with nothing. On the third cast his face betrayed nothing, but after reaching over the edge of the boat, he turned around with my dripping combo in his free hand. At that moment, I thought he could do just about anything.

"Just got to have the right hook," he laughed, and he untied that giant three-pronged monstrosity and put it back in the box where he'd found it.

The Business End

After choosing a rod and a reel, your next stop in the tackle shop will be that dizzying display of doo-hickeys, the terminal tackle section.

The business end of a fishing line is called the terminal tackle, and your choice of leader, sinker and hook can mean the difference between a hamburger for supper and a fish dinner. Guides on the coast all say less is better.

"Those store-bought pre-rigged things are fine, but my advice is that the less junk you've got on the line the better off you're going to be," A-Team Fishing's Bobby Abruscato said. "If you're serious, you want to help your chances catching fish. Especially in this water that stays so clear, those fish are going to get a good look at everything, so keep it simple, as simple as you can in terminal tackle."

Remember that those pre-rigged single- or double-drop leaders you'll see on the shelf, when used properly, can catch fish, but in some conditions they can also scare fish away. Inshore Guide Captain Jeff Chambliss puts it bluntly.

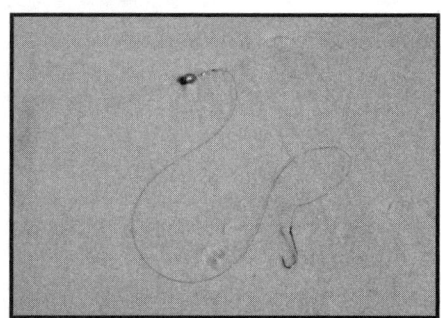

Guides say a Carolina rig like this one will be the most useful terminal tackle rig in the Gulf Shores and Orange Beach area.

"We call those 'tour-on' rigs: moron tourist rigs. They sell like crazy, but it's way too much crap on the tackle. You don't need red beads, you just need a hook, a leader, a swivel and little lead," he said.

What Chambliss and literally every guide on the coast recommend is the venerable Carolina rig, a simple-to-tie bottom rig that consists of just what Chambliss mentioned: an egg-weight, a swivel, and a hook on the end of a leader line. "Ninety percent of the fishing I do is on a Carolina rig," Bay Ranger Captain Frank Ford said.

Let's start with sinkers.

Sinkers

Your weight serves two functions: it's what you throw when you cast, and it's what

Brain teaser: What weighs more, a one-ounce lead weight or a one-ounce tungsten weight?

keeps your bait where it'll attract fish. Form follows function, and the egg-weight does both jobs perfectly when it's tied on a Carolina rig. Outfit yourself with a few different sizes to be prepared for faster currents that can push your bait away from where you want it or conditions that demand a longer cast.

For most conditions, guides say a 3/8- to half-ounce egg weight is perfect. "If I was pitching from the beach," Gulf Adventures' Captain DeJuan Tedder said, "I'd use a 3/8- to a half-ounce sinker." Tedder's advice is echoed across the board, though many captains note that unusually fast shore currents can require a weight with a different form.

Ford said he'll go up to a one-ounce sinker if conditions require it, but if the current is still bucking your bait, guides say, tie on a pyramid sinker rig. Captain Ted Childress explains,

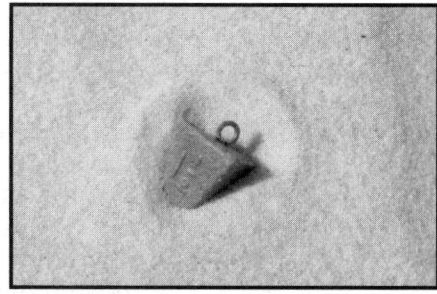

The shape of a pyramid weight helps it to dig into a sandy bottom and stay put in a heavy-running current.

"If they're fishing for whiting or pompano, a lot of beach fishermen use a pyramid sinker because it will dig down in the sand and won't move. They come off it with a two-foot long leader with a hook on the end, a J-hook or treble hook or a circle hook. They just put the bait on there and let it sit."

For most conditions, then, a selection of egg weights from 3/8- to 1-ounce in addition to some 1-ounce pyramid weights will fill your terminal tackle needs in the area of sinkers. You'll also need barell swivels to keep your line from being twisted as the current moves your bait, and you'll need to get some line to make your own leader to attach your hook.

Fishing FAQ:
Sinker weights
Which one weighs more? Here's a quick list of common sinker weights, from lightest to heaviest:
1/4 oz.
3/8 oz.
1/2 oz.
1 oz.

Leaders

Fishing in salt water opens up the possibility of catching a number of fish, big fish, or fish with a

If you're fishing on a budget, monofilament leader material is the most cost-effective choice.

feature some anglers have never come in contact with: sharp teeth. To deal with the challenges presented by fishing for saltwater game fish, anglers use a leader, a length of tougher line attached to the hook.

Leader material can make the difference in whether you catch fish or spend the day soaking bait. Leader material comes in several varieties, including wire, monofilament and fluorocarbon, and each has its own advantages and drawbacks.

Wire leaders resist abrasion from rocks or fish teeth that can weaken or sever your line, but they're highly visible to fish in the water. Fluorocarbon leaders are almost invisible in the water, and they're low-stretch lines, so you'll have greater sensitivity to light strikes, but they're more expensive than monofilament lines. Monofilament leaders stretch and absorb the shock of a heavy strike, but they're less abrasion resistant, so if you're not careful to examine your leader often you might lose a fish in the middle of a fight when your leader breaks.

Ideally, you'll have all three leader materials in your tackle box and be prepared for any situation. If you're fishing on a budget, though, 20-pound-test monofilament leader material is the most cost-effective combination of low-visibility, strength and durability. Buy enough to use it when you need it; about 50 yards is plenty.

Pro Tip: Check your line often, especially near the terminal tackle, for knicks or abrasions. Pinch it between your fingers as your reel in line to check your bait, feeling as you reel for rough places. Monofilament leader line is the same material as any other monofilament line, but it's wound on a larger spool to create larger memory coils to keep bait away from the sinker. You can reduce memory coils by stretching the line before you use it. Pull it enough to feel the spring in the line, but don't jerk it.

Hooks

Hooks come in a wide variety of sizes and shapes, but local guides agree that a No. 2 hook is just about perfect for shore fishing.

"A No. 2 to a 2/0 hook, depending on how big of a fish you're going for and the bait you're using, is what I like. Even if you're using a live bait or fishing for something big like speckled trout, usually a No. 2 hook is fine," Captain Jeff Chambliss of the Baby Therapy said.

Make sure to have enough hooks on hand before you go fishing, and get a

Hooks come in different sizes and shapes, and they're inexpensive tackle. You'll be well-prepared for most fish with, from left to right, J–hooks, treble hooks and circle hooks.

variety of styles. Sometimes a treble, or three-barbed hook, is more effective. Speckled trout expert Captain Yano Serra recommends a treble hook under some conditions.

"In the winter it's totally different than in the spring, and it's totally different in the summer, but that's when the bait's going to be live shrimp on a No. 8 or a No. 10 treble hook," Serra said.

Another option worth keeping in your tackle box is the circle hook. Its point curves toward the hook shank more than a J-hook and can catch fish when you don't pick up the strike and set the hook in time. "If you're (bottom) fishing (offshore) in the Gulf, a circle hook is required, but they're great to use from

Hook sizes
Single–point hook sizes are indicated using a two–part system. Hooks designed wtih a "No." get bigger as the number gets smaller. A hook designated with a "/0" gets bigger as the number gets larger. For example, hooks, from smaller to larger, include:
No. 3
No. 2
No. 1
1/0 ("One-aught")
2/0
3/0

shore too. You just start cranking when a fish hits it. There's no jerking involved," Bay Ranger Captain Frank Ford said.

Get a variety of hooks that includes treble, J-hooks and circle hooks, but keep in mind that size and color matter. A-Team Fishing's Captain Bobby Abruscato swears by dark-colored hooks.

"Keep your hooks dark. Get bronze hooks rather than big silver hooks. Even gold is better than silver hooks," he said.

Pro-Tip: Don't throw away the tiny plastic bag your hooks come packed in; keep your hooks in there until you're ready to tie them on. Loose hooks are harder to get out of fingers than they are fish's mouths.

Now you've got almost everything you'll need to hook into a fine fish from the shore: rod, reel, line, leader, sinkers, barell swivels and some hooks. Ready to fish yet? Good. In no time you'll be on the water with a bent rod, but before you leave the tackle shop you'll want a few more pieces of equipment to make the process go a little smoother.

Guides in the area say some pieces of equipment are "must-have."

You don't need a tacklebox filled with solutions to every problem to fish from shore; sinkers, hooks, swivels and leader material will be enough to get you catching fish.

Fish On! Shore: Gulf Shores/Orange Beach

III. Accessories

I only went shrimpin' with Granddaddy a few times. Shrimpin's not like fishing with a pole, which is relaxing, even-paced and leisurely. Shrimpin's work.

We'd put out Granddaddy's fiberglass V-hull that day under sunny skies and over calm water. Unlike other days, he'd let the motor idle when he'd arrived at where he'd put out the net. I did

A small cast net can be a great accessory. It can catch bait, or it might just catch supper.

my best to help him feed it over the back of the boat, but a little guy isn't much help at that kind of work.

We'd slowly pulled the net for a while, Granddaddy at the wheel, right hand on the throttle lever, and me next to him watching the wake the bow made and stretching my hand down to feel the water splashing.

When he'd gone far enough, Granddaddy cut the motor down to an

34

idle again and put the catch trough he'd constructed across the mid-section of the boat. It was an open-topped box about three feet wide with six-inch walls and a wooden gate in a slot at one end. I'd never seen it used, and I was fascinated when he pulled the net back into the boat and released its contents into the trough.

I saw things I'd never imagined existed. Slithering eels, a host of blue crabs, tiny shad and puffer fish blown up like tiny balloons and covered with skin that stretched into flexible spikes.

I saw things I'd never imagined existed. Slithering eels, a host of blue crabs, tiny shad and puffer fish blown up like tiny balloons and covered with skin that stretched into flexible spikes. And shrimp, a fantastic amount of shrimp, peppered the wet, slick bottom of the enclosure that stretched from one side of the boat to the other.

In my family, shrimp has a special place. On Christmas we eat ham like everyone else, and on Thanksgiving it's turkey, but on anyone's birthday, or when family comes in from out of town to visit, it's fried shrimp. I can't remember when I learned how to peel them; I'd guess I was born knowing. Back in those days we didn't even de-vein them. Just pinch the head and hold onto the tail and pull.

On that first run I watched Granddaddy pick through what seemed to me like one or two of everything that could live in the water, grabbing the shrimp and tossing them into a five-gallon bucket. On the next drag I began to help, mindful of his warnings to be

Fish On! Shore: Gulf Shores/Orange Beach

careful of anything with teeth or claws. Our bucket was filling with shrimp and a nice batch of blue crabs. When we'd picked out all the shrimp he'd pull up the gate on one end of the trough and tip everything else back into the water, helping any reluctant hangers-on back home with a scrap of wood he'd brought for just that purpose.

On the third drag I'd done my best to help pull the heavy net up, and I watched the catch trough eagerly as he positioned the net above it, poised to start picking out shrimp from the writhing mass of living creatures. As he shook the net after filling the trough I watched one more thing fall out and begin the most ferocious flopping I'd seen in my young life.

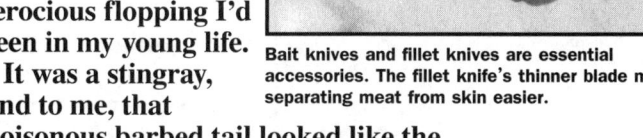

Bait knives and fillet knives are essential accessories. The fillet knife's thinner blade makes separating meat from skin easier.

It was a stingray, and to me, that poisonous barbed tail looked like the pointiest, scariest thing I'd ever seen.

I can remember my mouth falling open, and, more than stepping backward, feeling the sensation of the edge of the boat striking my backside. I flung my hands behind me and literally pushed up on the gunnel, thinking, I guess, that going over the side would be a better option than sticking around with that fearsome creature.

With only an inch or so left before I'd fall off the boat backward like a scuba diver, I looked wide-eyed over at

Granddaddy. Calmly, as if by reflex, he'd reached behind him and grabbed his bait knife. His arm moved in a flash, and the point came down on the hard wooden trough with a wet thud. The stingray pinned underneath it continued to wiggle and thrash that tail I was sure could kill either one of us. Without a word, Granddaddy pried the tip free, and with a flick of his wrist flipped the stingray over the side.

From that day on, I've always fished with a knife handy.

Must-Have Equipment

What kind of accessory equipment is critical for fishing in salt water? Some things are optional, guides say, especially if you're not looking to break the bank on tackle and equipment, but some things are worth every penny.

Take a hook removal device.

"If you're using live bait you can get a flow-troll bait bucket, something you can keep in the water to keep the bait alive, and you'll want to have a stringer, especially if you're going to move up and down the beach," A-Team Fishing's Bobby Abruscato said. "You'll want to have a bait knife and a good set of needle-nosed pliers."

"You need something to unhook

Ice chests
Whether you call it an ice chest or a cooler, having some way to keep things cold is a must. If you do what this book advises, you'll need a big one! Generally, a 48-quart cooler is sufficient, but if you've carrying a lot of drinks you might want a separate ice chest for fish.

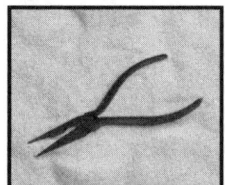

Hook removal devices serve the same purpose as needle–nosed pliers: they make getting your terminal tackle back from a toothy fish safer and easier.

catfish or toothy critters," Captain Jeff Chambliss warns. "Needle-nosed pliers are an invaluable tool. Most people coming from fresh water don't realize just how bad a saltwater catfish sting is."

Abruscato advises getting a small tackle box to keep your terminal tackle, but, he said, it doesn't have to be expensive, and any container will do in a pinch. "You'll want to have at least a Tupperware container for your terminal tackle. You can get a little Plano tackle box for next to nothing that can handle all your extra

Tide charts are presented in a variety of ways, and they're available for free courtesy of the State of Alabama. You'll also find them published in local newspapers.

hooks, weights and swivels," he said. "You don't want to have to run back up to the condo every time you break off a rig to get another weight."

Veteran guide Captain Don Holloway of the Back Bay offers some wise advice about equipment to land a fish.

"You've got to land it, and that means a net. A lot of people will buy a hand gaff (a large hook to snag a fish out of the water), but it's hard to gaff a smaller fish," Holloway said. "You just need a little long-handled net, something with about a four-foot handle. Even a kiddie net will work."

Holloway offers another gem that can keep your trip on the right side of the law. "In Alabama the state publishes a tide chart calendar with a bar graph of

Landing Net Tips
• Don't bring the net to the fish, bring the fish, head-first, to the net.
• Don't put the net in the water until you're ready to lead the fish into the net. Nets can snag hooks and allow fish to get away.
• If you're landing the fish yourself, keep tension on the line by holding the rod at arm's length in your dominant hand. That will avoid putting too much bend in the rod at its tip where it could break.

the tides for every day of the year. Inside it's got pictures of all the game fish in the water and all the size limits and bag limits and all the info you'll need to stay out of trouble," he said. Even better, that tide chart calendar is free.

Bait and tackle shops sell rulers and tape measures to ensure you're within the letter of the law on size limits for game fish. "You'll need that tape measure," Holloway said. "Marine Police and the Game and Fish wardens, when they say '14-inch speckled trout' they don't mean 13-and-a-half-inches. They don't want to see that. That's the law, and you need to comply with that."

If you have any questions about size limits or bag limits, most bait shops will be happy to answer them. "You don't want to drop a grand on a game and fish law violation," Holloway said, "just because you didn't know. I've had people come up to me with an ice chest full of fish and ask if I know which ones are good eating, and I look inside and it's full of undersize fish, game and fish law violations. The key is to know, and if you violate that and get caught you've got no one to blame but yourself."

Ignorance is no excuse
Game and fish laws are no joke, and it's up to you to know the rules. You can get a list of creel and size limits at most bait and tackle stores, or you can download complete regulations from the Alabama Department of Conservation and Natural Resources website at www.outdooralabama.com/fishing/saltwater/regulations/

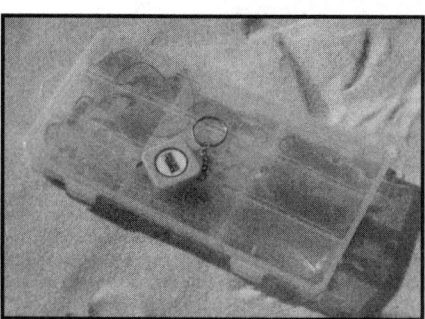

Tape measures and fish rulers can keep you out of trouble with fish and game regulations on the minimum or maximum keeper sizes for fish.

Hook removal tools, bait knives and bait buckets (even aerators for ice chests or bait buckets are reasonably priced), landing nets and measuring tools are must-haves, guides say, in addition to a stringer or a cooler to keep your catch until you clean it. Other tools, they say, may or may not be useful to you. The Audrey II's Captain David Brown mentions a few useful items.

"A bait that's becoming more popular is the ghost shrimp, but you have to have a suction tube to get them out of the sand. You push this PVC pipe in the sand, and then suction the sand and the ghost shrimp in it and then pump it out," he said.

"It all depends on the level of seriousness you're going to go to. If you're going to get up early and get ready to go, you'll probably want to have (bait catching equipment) available to you. Another thing is the rod holder, a PVC pipe about three feet long you can get at any beach shop. Also, some of the basic stuff like sunscreen, polarized sunglasses and a hat. A fishing license: you've got to have that. You might want to have a pair of gloves."

Another basic no tackle box on the beach should be without is meat tenderizer. Use it to counteract jellyfish stings.

Some equipment you'll find in the tackle store, especially equipment you

"A bait that's becoming more popular is the ghost shrimp, but you have to have a suction tube to get them. You push this PVC pipe in the sand and then suction the sand and the ghost shrimp in it."

can use to catch your own bait (for a more detailed discussion of bait-catching equipment see the chapter on bait), can add to your fishing experience. Children, for example, often enjoy catching bait more than catching edible fish. Though our tackle stores are run by professionals who've forgotten more about fishing than most people know, they might not always be quick to give decisive answers about specific products. Some products are either beyond the scope of a beginner or as-yet unproven tools. Don't be mad; they're just being honest. As with everything, let the buyer beware.

Now that you're outfitted like a seasoned old salt you're ready for the last stop before you hit the water: the bait section!

IV. Bait & Rigs

The last thing we'd do on the way out the door was grab the bait. Granddaddy kept a bag in the freezer with cut bait: croakers, shad or small white trout from the last trip.

We never stopped at the bait store on the way, to be honest, and, truth be told, I saw Granddaddy turn his nose up at a box of frozen cigar minnows more than once.

"I saw Granddaddy turn his nose up at a box of frozen cigar minnows more than once."

If worst came to worst, Granddaddy could always find some bait, at least enough to start out the day and catch some more. I was a little surprised the day I first learned how he did it.

We'd put the boat in and started motoring slowly toward our fishing area when he stopped.

"Got to get some bait," he said. Until then I hadn't noticed that the only thing he'd pulled out of the freezer that morning was a frozen 1-gallon milk jug of ice.

I reached for a pole, unsure of what, exactly, he had in mind. He reached down from his seat near the outboard in the back of the boat and grabbed the galvanized tin bucket that held his cast net as he rose and picked his way toward the bow.

Standing there on the tossing bow, he threw a few feet of the cast net edge over his right arm and put another section of it in his mouth. Granddaddy's cast nets are worth explaining a little. I would watch him patch one or tie a new one for hours. Sitting there in the barn door, he'd work the green plastic net needle over and over, hands moving through the motions of tying the evenly-spaced knots with practiced ease. I asked him once to show me how he did it, but he'd just tell me to watch as he'd demonstrate another knot, hands moving faster than my eyes could follow. He'd work for hours on a new net, and, when he'd finished a new 12-footer, he'd get some rope and start stringing weights. Uncle Gary would have to tell you about casting them in the forge Great-granddaddy built in the shop next to the barn. All that happened long before I was born, but Granddaddy never let a piece of scrap lead get past him. We've still got plenty if we ever need more weights.

Until then, I'd never seen Granddaddy

Sitting there in the barn door, he'd work the green plastic net needle over and over.

use the cast net for bait. He'd trade his brogans for a pair of old black sneakers and wade between the piers on the inland side of Orange Beach, piers that were sparse in those days, and throw the cast net for mullet. Some people will tell you mullet is no good for eating, but I'll knock you down to get to a smoked mullet. I thought the cast net was an eatin'-fish tool. Bait was what you caught in-between catching fish for the table or the freezer.

Sabiki rigs work with your main rod–and–reel combo, a smaller combo dedicated to bait fishing or even by hand.

Now cast-netting is an art, not a science, and I'll admit it's an art I never mastered. Gary can do it better than I can, but he'll readily admit he's not as proficient at it as Granddaddy was. Standing there on the bow of that rocking boat with a salty edge of net in his mouth and the tether rope tied around his wrist, Granddaddy looked like an Olympic athlete at the top of his game when he'd cast his net. He'd turn at the waist and take a deep breath and swing around, slow at first and then faster, and at just the right moment he'd release first one hand, then the other, somewhere in there letting go with his clenched teeth, and the net, like it couldn't help but do it any other way, would spring out into a perfect circle, a tiny spray of water flung from its wet rope edge, and hit the surface and sink beneath another perfect circle that

44

spread in an ever-widening ripple in all directions.

We caught some shad that day and moved on to fishing, catching more bait as we did and never running out. We even had some left to save in the freezer for next time.

> *"Maybe one day, I thought, I'd teach my own son how to do it and pass along the skill."*

Later in life, when Granddaddy had come to the point that he'd passed throwing the cast net, I planned to get a recorder and hide it on me somewhere and ask him, make him, show me exactly how to work that green plastic net needle. I'd get him, I thought, to explain it in great detail in his own words and in his own voice, and I'd have it to save forever. Maybe one day, I thought, I'd teach my own son how to do it and pass along the skill. I mentioned it once after Granddaddy had asked me laughingly if I'd seen how much they charged for cast nets, little bitty ones, in stores. He seemed agreeable, though more interested in other things.

The day I got the call that Granddaddy had died I walked down to the edge of the lake I lived next to, the closest body of water I could find. Through my tears and among all my other thoughts and memories I recalled my plan to get Granddaddy to teach me to tie cast nets, and I cried, in part, that I'd never really done it.

I'd waited too long. I'd missed my chance.

I've still got tears for that.

Fish On! Shore: Gulf Shores/Orange Beach

The Best Bait

Any discussion of bait for saltwater fishing begins and ends with shrimp. "You'll never go wrong with shrimp," A-Team Fishing's Captain Bobby Abruscato said. "Of the top three baits to use when salt water fishing, the first one on the list is shrimp, any kind, live or dead, but I prefer live shrimp."

Bait comes, basically, in three categories, live, dead or cut.

Live Bait

To me, the fish seem to like the bait to be alive," Gulf Adventures' Captain DeJuan Tedder said. "Sport fish are a little harder to catch, fish like speckled trout or flounder, but you can catch them, especially if you've got live bait. It works better because they're ambush fish."

A flow–troll bait bucket is a great way to keep live bait alive. Make sure to grab several feet of rope from the tackle store to make a tether for it.

Live shrimp are often available at bait shops, and it's simple to keep bait alive and fresh when fishing: just make sure to keep the bait in oxygen-rich water. Use a flow-troll bait bucket, or buy a battery-powered aerator to make any bucket or cooler filled with salt water into a live well. "Just don't put ten dozen in there," Holloway laughs. "Put three dozen in there, and, if you have to, run back and get some more."

Captain David Brown of the Audrey II said live shrimp are his number one bait, though they do require more attention than some other baits.

"As far as bait, I prefer live shrimp, but it's high-maintenance. A lot of little stuff will nibble on it, so it's hard to put out there and leave it," Brown said. Other live baits are less soft-bodied and easier to fish.

A battery-powered aerator keeps water in a bucket or ice chest oxygenated and bait alive.

"If you want to purchase a cast net you can obtain free bait like menhaden or bull minnows," Bay Ranger Captain Frank Ford said. "A five-foot net is plenty big enough, and you can catch finger mullet and may even end up catching supper."

Baby Therapy's Captain Jeff Chambliss noted that many small fish species work well as live bait. "If you've got a cast net or a sabiki rig you can catch pogies, croakers, or pilchards."

Shad: A.K.A. Menhaden, shiners, pogies
Croaker: A.K.A. finger mullet
Hardtail: A.K.A. Blue runner, yellow jack

Two species of bait fish are important to mention here. Shad, also called Menhaden or pogies, are a common bait fish, and you can often spot schools driven to the surface by game fish below. Croakers, notable for the croaking sound they make when caught and taken out of the water, are great live bait as well.

"If I'm going big, I go with a big

croaker," Captain Yano Serra of Spectacklelures said. "If I can get a croaker as big as one pound, I'll use him. That'll catch anywhere from a six- to an eight- or nine-pound fish."

Cut Bait

Anything you catch that isn't good eating can be used as cut bait, though some bait is more appetizing than others to fish.

"If you start catching small fish you can use that as cut bait," Abruscato said. Cut bait has the advantage of being as fresh as bait can be, and it's guaranteed to be the natural food source for fish in the very water you're working.

"It makes light years of difference when you're using fresh bait."

Croaker, pinfish, shad, hardtail, and a whole host of almost any fish that swims can make good cut bait. The key, as with any bait, is freshness.

"You need fresh bait, whether live or dead, versus frozen," Abruscato said. "It makes light years of difference when you're using fresh bait. Ask if it's been frozen or not, and spend the extra money to get fresh bait."

Croaker is a fantastic bait, and you'll recognize one by the sound it makes when it's pulled out of the water. Though it's a great baitfish, it comes out pretty good fried, too.

Dead Bait

Squid is a bait that carries mixed reviews, and it falls into the dead bait category. "Squid is probably a close second," Abruscato said, "Again, make sure it's fresh. You're not going to go wrong if you use fish (cut bait) or squid, but it's important, and I can't emphasize it enough, that it be fresh."

Captain David Brown falls into the anti-squid camp. Though tougher than shrimp (and easier to fish since it won't get taken off the hook), squid has drawbacks like attracting hardhead catfish and being less appetizing to sport fish than shrimp.

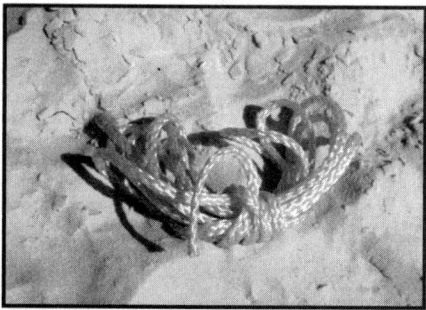

A length of good rope can be invaluable when fishing from the shore. Use it to secure your flow-troll bucket to your rod-holder or tie it to your waist if you're wade-fishing.

"I would never go with squid," Brown said. "I'm not saying you can't catch anything on it, but I would never do that. Ask someone around the bait shop, and get something else. Fiddler crabs or sand fleas are good dead bait."

A great tip for using dead bait comes from Captain Don Holloway. Make salted shrimp.

"Buy some dead shrimp and pinch the head and the tail off and peel off the skin," Holloway said. Lay the bait on a single layer of newspaper and cover it with table salt and let it sit overnight. The salt pulls all the moisture out and toughens up the bait, and that's excellent bait in the surf. It's what the fish are looking for: food particles washing around in the current."

It's worth noting that artificial lures work just as well in salt water as in fresh water. Top-water or diving plugs, plastic grubs or spoons are all effective if they're targeted toward the conditions on the water and a particular species of fish. The variety available makes the subject far too entailed to go into here, but tackle store proprietors will be happy to point you toward lures that are proven in local waters if you're interested in going that route.

"Squid is probably a close second. Again, make sure it's fresh. You're not going to go wrong if you use fish (cut bait) or squid, but it's important, and I can't emphasize it enough, that it be fresh."

In short, bait selection is another decision that can make or break your fishing trip. Guides advise you select the right bait for the fish you're trying to catch.

"You've got to have the right bait for the right fish," Captain Don Holloway said. "A lot of people will go buy bait, and some people catch pinfish, but you have to realize that a bigger bait is for bigger fish. You have to get the fish to bite the bait."

Which brings us back to shrimp. "Everything in the Gulf eats shrimp," Holloway chuckles.

50

Obtaining Bait

Bait etiquette
It's no problem if you have to ask a fellow angler for some bait if you run out, but only after you run out. Don't show up to fish without bait and expect someone to bail you out. The other side of the coin is true, too: if another fisherman needs some bait, give him some! Finally, if you've got bait left at the end of the day, try and give it to someone so it'll be put to use. Good deeds always come back to you.

Buying bait at the bait and tackle store is probably the best way to obtain bait since it's a good time to ask questions. "One of the best things you can do is go to the tackle store," Childress Charters' Captain Ted Childress said. "If you start asking the right questions, if you know what kind of fish you're going for, you can get even more knowledge."

Bait shops can often tell you what bait has been working well recently in the water you're fishing, but for more adventurous anglers, catching your own bait is a good move, though you should be aware that it's another skill to master.

"Something like that may be a little much," Abruscato said. "If you want to try to catch your own bait, though, get a five-foot cast net, or get some bream hooks and try to catch the fish you want to use as bait, fish like pinfish, croakers or sweet trout."

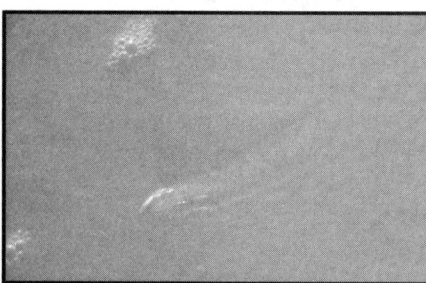

Sand fleas burrow beneath the surface in the impact zone where the waves wash up on the beach. They strain passing water for food particles, creating V-shaped signs like those pictured above.

An option similar to using bream hooks is the sabiki rig. Simply tie this multi-hooked rig on, drop it near a seawall or around some pilings and jig it up and down. Pinfish are often visible near the surface, and with a little practice you can catch more than one at a time.

Sand fleas make great bait for many fish off the shore, and though you can dig them out of the sand with your hands, a sand flea rake available at the bait or tackle shop makes the process a little easier. Just look for the V-shaped wake the sand flea makes in the zone where the waves hit the shore, and scoop them from two to four inches beneath the surface.

Catching bait can save a few dollars, and it's a fun (and useful) pastime for children. Though certainly worth it, it may, however, cost more time away from fishing than you're willing to give.

"It can be a big expense to catch your own live bait," Gulf Adventures' DeJuan Tedder said, "And if you don't have a clue about how to do it or you're unsure, you can find a local tackle store and buy bait. There's a ton of them in the area."

Sabiki rigs and sand flea scoops are two bait–catching tools you many want to have available.

Rigs

The number one rig for salt water fishing from the shore is the tried-and-true Carolina rig referred to earlier. Baby Therapy Captain Jeff Chambliss describes it.

"Most of the time your rig will be a Carolina rig: a half-ounce slip lead (egg sinker) tied behind a swivel and the other side of the swivel tied to a foot-and-a-half of leader and that tied to up to a 2/0 hook, depending on how big the fish and the bait you're using are."

To tie on a Carolina rig, slip an egg

weight on your main line and tie the main line to a barrel swivel. Tie 18 to 24 inches of leader material, 20-pound test monofilament line, to the other side of the barrel swivel. At the end of the leader material tie on your No. 2 hook. The Carolina rig is a bottom rig designed to allow the bait to drift in the current a few inches to a few feet from the bottom, and the egg weight allows line to slip past it and the bait to move naturally with the current where the fish can see it.

Fishing FAQ:
Presentation: Anglers call the movement of the bait they create using both water current and retrieve speed the bait's presentation. Understanding the feeding habits of the fish species you're targeting will aid your efforts to present the bait in a way that triggers strikes.

"If you're trying to get on the bottom, a Carolina rig, an egg weight with a swivel, is all you need," Back Bay Captain Don Holloway said.

When using a Carolina rig, the purpose of the weight is to keep the bait in one place. If the current pulls your bait around too much, move up from a 3/8-ounce weight to a half-ounce size. If you're still fighting a strong current, you may want to tie on a single-drop bottom rig.

The Carolina rig is a bottom rig that works when fishing for a wide variety of species. If you could only use one rig when fishing saltwater, this would be it.

To tie a single-drop bottom rig, use a three-way swivel instead of a barrel swivel to tie on a pyramid sinker. Tie your main line to one eye, and use a two-foot section of line to extend your line to an end where you'll tie the pyramid sinker. Use the remaining eye to tie your 18- to 24-inch leader, and end it with a No. 2 hook.

These rigs work great with both live and dead bait, and the best knot to use in every application is called the Uni knot. If you had to use only one knot for fishing applications, the Uni knot is the one you should know how to tie.

Tying a Uni knot takes three steps. Take it one step at a time, and you'll be tying it like a pro before you know it.

First, thread the end of your line through the eye of your hook or your swivel, and pinch both parts of the line, the one leading to the hook and the one leading away from it, between your thumb and forefinger. Now you've created a double section of line a few inches in length between the hook or swivel and your fingers. Complete the first step of tying the knot by forming a loop under the double section. Form the loop by bringing the free end of the line back toward the hook or swivel and passing it over the doubled line. Take a look at the top illustration on this page to see how this step should look.

Next, wrap the free end of the line

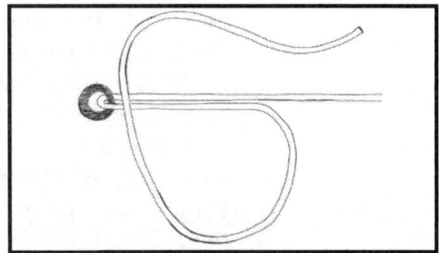

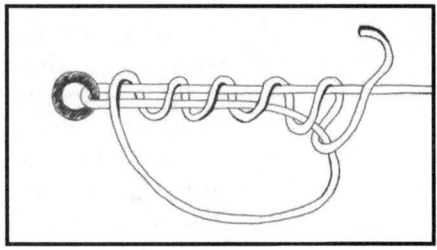

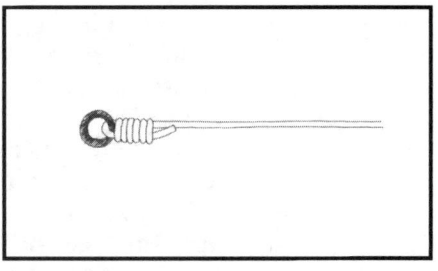

A Uni knot is the best knot to use when tying on hooks, leaders or lead. It maintains the strength of the line better than most knots.

around the doubled section by pulling it behind the doubled section and toward yourself. The line should wrap around the doubled section but not the loop you created in step one. Continue to wrap the free end around the doubled section at least four times. Make sure you pass the free end through the loop you created in step one, not around it. When you're finished wrapping the doubled section, pass the free end through the loop and out toward the line side of your knot. The middle illustration on page 53 shows how this step should look.

Finally, lubricate the the wrapping with some saliva, and pull the free end to tighten the knot. Pull the line while holding the hook to make the knot slip down the line toward the hook or swivel until the knot is snug against the eye. The finished knot should look like the bottom illustration on page 53 now.

Knots and rigging terminal tackle are probably the single most daunting area of fishing for those who've never done it. Don't be afraid to practice tying knots, and remember, everyone has to learn sometime. If you have trouble, try using your mouth as a third hand to hold the free end of the line during the tying process. Keeping the hook or the swivel on the same side every time you tie the knot, and tying it the same way every time will help you get more comfortable tying rigs.

Congratulations! You're ready to fish. Now, to find them!

V. When and Where

Well, I guess we won't be catching much today," Granddaddy said.

It was just after lunch, and we'd decided to take the boat out and do some fishing. The summer air barely moved, and I was putting my elbow out the window and looking out at the fields as we passed just like Granddaddy. He'd poured himself a cup of coffee from his ever-present Thermos by setting the cup in a roll of duct tape on the seat placed there just for that purpose, and after draining it he'd hung his elbow out the window again, his right hand resting lightly on the steering wheel and his head moving back and forth from the road to the fields as they unfolded in front of us.

"You think the wind's blowing the wrong direction?" I asked him. I remembered him telling me once that "Wind out of the east is when the fish bite the least. Wind out of the west, fish bite the best."

"Nope."

56

"Does the moon affect the fish during the day?" I wondered aloud.

"Naw, that ain't it."

"Think it's going to rain?" I was running out of reasons, but he seemed sure of himself.

"Naw, we ain't gonna get any rain."

"Well, then, what is it?"

"Cows are lying down."

"The cows?" Ridiculous, I thought.

"Yep. If the cows ain't eatin', the fish liable won't be either," he said, and he looked over the bench seat at me as if he wondered if I'd believe him. I never got him to admit if he was pulling my leg.

But, if I recall our luck correctly, he was right.

We didn't catch much that day.

When

Every guide on the coast agrees, the best time for fishing is whenever you can go fishing. "A lot of days the wind is from the east," Bay Ranger Captain Frank Ford mused. "We get wind from the east more than we do anything else. You just have to go fishing. I've caught them on an east wind."

Wind can have a lot to do with when fishing is the best, Childress Charters' Captain Ted Childress said, especially in the winter. "Bull redfish season starts in late October and runs through February or sometime in March. The peak of it is around Thanksgiving to mid-January," he said. "You can catch them off the shoreline at that time of year, and usually it's best right after a

Be Observant!
Most public beaches have color-coded flags that indicate surf conditions, and most are visible from quite a distance. If you're observant, you'll even note which direction the wind is blowing the flag.

Green flag: Low hazard (Calm conditions)
Yellow flag: Medium hazard (Moderate surf/currents)
Red Flag: High hazard (High surf/strong currents)
Double Red Flags: Water closed to the public (It's illegal to enter the water when double red flags are being flown.)

cold front. When it's blowing hard you might think the conditions are terrible, but when that north wind's blowing, that's when they bite the most."

In general, however, moving water is more important to get fish biting than moving air. "As long as the tide's moving, period," Gulf Adventures' Captain DeJuan Tedder said. "I've done better than at any other time an hour to two hours after it starts moving. Watch the water, and look for the movement. Throw a float out and see if the water's moving."

Tides move debris, seaweed and shells, to the highest point on the beach the water reaches. You can tell roughly where the tide is in its cycle by looking for the high tide mark.

Moving water, whether it's caused by current or tide, guides say, is key to catching fish.

"If you're fishing in a pass or on the Intercoastal Canal, the tide makes the water move, and that's something that turns the fish on," Ford said. "If it's running hard outgoing or hard incoming, either one will have more water moving, and most of the time that makes the fish bite better."

Structure matters! Water will move faster through a tight, constrained space than an open area.

Captain Don Holloway explains that tide or current movement makes bait fish move, and that's what makes fish bite.

"On the beach, you'll fish the incoming or outgoing tide; it doesn't matter as long as it's moving and the bait is moving around," Captain Holloway said. Baby Therapy Captain

Jeff Chambliss echoed Holloway's advice, and added that the more the water's moving, the better.

"There's a 12-hour gap between the tides, and the best time to fish is whenever you've got time to go, but it's better if there's some tide moving," Chambliss said. "You want some moving water. Right at high tide or before high tide can be the best time, and a lot of times at the end of an outgoing tide it's usually kind of crummy. At the beginning of an outgoing tide it's usually great for the first few hours of it."

Chambliss added that daybreak and dusk are good times to catch fish.

"The best time to fish is whenever you've got time to go, but it's better if there's some tide moving."

One of Spectacklelures' Captain Yano Serra's favorite times to fish is early morning. "In the mornings, I start out throwing top water. You'll catch some big fish and lots of them when you get in the middle of them," he said.

A-Team Fishing's Captain Bobby Abruscato swears by daybreak fishing. "In this area, dealing with the clear water we have here, the best time, no matter what the season or tide, is right at daybreak. That's the best window of fishing opportunity right there." Abruscato said water movement not only stirs up bait, it can get fish to home in on your bait.

"The water moving will transfer the scent of the bait through the water," he said. "If you can, time that (daybreak) around when you're having the tide move, especially around when it's changing, coming in or going out, and that'll help your chances to land fish."

Put simply: Fish when the water is moving the bait, and you'll probably catch fish. Remember, though, it's never a bad time to go fishing.

Where to Fish

Gulf Shores and Orange Beach are full of places that hold fish, and literally every square yard of water could hold a great fish for you to catch. So where do you wet your line if you're looking to maximize your chances at hooking up?

"You can pretty much fish anywhere along the beach, but if you find a point or some structure, or if you know where to find some old structure on the

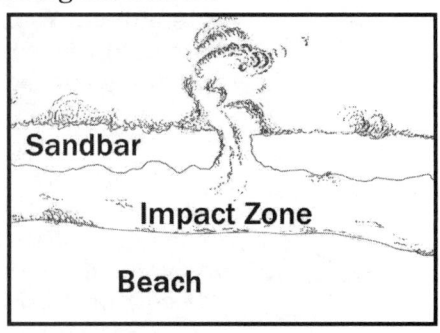

Wave action forms characteristic structures on most beaches including an impact zone and a sandbar. Recognizing beach structure will help you identify places more likely to hold fish.

beach it helps," Gulf Adventures' Captain DeJuan Tedder said. The experts all advise finding some structure in the water that will hold bait fish.

Alabama Department of Conservation and Natural Resources' Marine Resources Division Chief Marine Biologist Kevin Anson characterizes the shoreline habitat as one dominated by smooth bottoms and wave energy.

"The front beach is a sandy habitat, and typically a high-energy habitat," he said. "At the shoreline the waves form bars where most of the energy is captured as those waves break. There will be at least a first bar and maybe a second bar, and that energy provides an opportunity for folks tuned in to what the habitat is making the fish do."

Structure, like a sandbar, for example, is key to success, Bay Ranger Captain Frank Ford said.

Why Structure?
Structure affects currents, allowing fish to swim more easily and expend less energy. In the natural world, energy must be maintained by feeding, and obtaining food isn't always so easy. Why else? Watch the people around you. Everything naturally responds to its environment. If there was only one tree in a sunny field, where would you stand?

"On the beach, any kind of structure helps, and sometimes the only structure there will be represented by a break on the sandbar. At an inlet or at a pass, you might find some rocks, or jetties, something out there that's different that can hold bait," Ford said. "Anything out there that's different, a different shape on the bottom, something that people have taken out and put on the bottom, some type of structure, will be a fish attraction device."

"Look for those areas of shoreline where there are a lot of waves, where water is getting pushed back out into the sea," Anson said. "Those outflows concentrate fish. The areas where food gets moved back offshore is where the fish will be waiting for it."

Along the coast, the term structure can refer to submerged objects like pilings from old piers, logs or old seawalls, but it can also refer to features on the bottom like troughs, sand bars or drop-off ledges. Don't be fooled into thinking fish only swim far from shore, either.

"If you're fishing on the beach, look

for pockets of deeper, darker water," Captain David Brown of the Audrey II said. "Look along the edges of the sandbar. The fish aren't necessarily in places where you have to cast a hundred yards. A lot of times the best fish are caught from 20 to 40 feet from the water line in the impact zone where the bait is stirred up by the wave action."

On the beach itself, the sandbar is the most important structural feature in the water. Captain Bobby Abruscato said you'll do yourself a favor to get a good look at it.

"If you have the opportunity, if you have an upstairs room, look out at the water," he said. "There's a sand bar that runs the length of the coast parallel to the beach, and there are places where that bar is a little further out, a little farther away from the beach. Particularly from the beach those little indentations actually create a feature that can hold fish. Any time you can find a feature like that, or a log or something on the bottom that can hold fish you'll have a better opportunity to catch something serious. Look for points, places that are washed out. If you see anything from the condo, any little feature, anything can make fish congregate and hold fish."

Captain Don Holloway said your best source for structural feature information may be a lifeguard. "If you ask a lifeguard where there's an undertow you might learn how to recognize where one is," Holloway said. "Where you see foam running out from shore, that's a cut in the sandbar, and

Reading Water
You'll thank yourself for learning to read the water you're fishing. Watch for the Three Cs: color, current and critters. Color can tell you about the water's depth; the darker it is the deeper it is. Current indicates whether bait is moving in the water and whether fish will be feeding or not. Critters can include birds, which often feed on similar bait fish to game fish, or bait fish themselves.

that's where the fish are because that's where the bait is. Everything that's washed up on the beach washes out with the undertow, and that's where you'll want to fish."

Something to note is that undertow, or rip tide, areas, are dangerous places to be in the water. When Holloway says "everything" gets washed out to sea, that means fishermen, too. It's a good rule to remember that moving water can move bait, but it can also move fishermen. Safety should always be your first priority. The next concern is, again, structure.

"It's all about structure," Holloway said. "Pilings, rocks, sunken boats or cuts in the sandbar or ledges or an irregular bottom. If you don't see that cut where the undertow pulls the water going out, then look at the water color and see the sandbar. See the lightness of the color of the water, and fish just inside it where the water gets a deeper, darker color. That's where the fish are."

Baby Therapy Captain Jeff Chambliss said the trough on the shore side of the sandbar is a great place to fish, and he added his

Structure is the most important element of choosing a location to fish. Anything different on the bottom, from drop-offs to sandbars to old pilings like the ones above can hold baitfish and game fish.

voice to the guides that advise looking for rip tide areas. Sometimes two sand bars form off the beach, he added.

"Look for a deep trough in the surf," he said. "Better yet, look for where the trough comes down to the beach. Find a spot where there's a break in the second bar where the water's flowing in and out and pushed by the waves falling on the beach and looking for a way to go, looking for a way out."

Any structure on the bottom might hold fish, Anson said. "Along passes, right there where the mouth of the pass is at the drop-off, for example at Fort Morgan where there's a significant drop-off, are places where people will drift baits along those edges. Red drum (redfish), primarily, but black drum, too, can be caught there. One feature you'll want to be on the lookout for is drop-offs. Where the water's clear enough to see those features, any hole or deeper water will concentrate fish."

It's a good rule to remember that moving water can move bait, but it can also move unwary fishermen. Safety should always be your first priority. The next concern is, again, structure.

One more tip for choosing a place to fish is to watch what birds are doing. "Sometimes you can just watch for birds feeding. Where fish are feeding, they'll have bait pushed to the surface where birds can access them," Ford said.

The Best Spots

Two places in the Gulf Shores/Orange Beach area draw praise as shore-fishing hot spots: The Gulf State Park Pier and Perdido Pass/Alabama Point.

The Gulf State Park Pier is one of the best values for fishing in Gulf Shores and Orange Beach.

"It's amazing the value you can get from fishing at the Gulf State Park Pier," Captain Ted Childress said. "You'll catch anything from flounder to sheepshead to pompano to redfish and speckled trout or King Mackerel and Spanish Mackerel. At the pier, probably the best time of the year is March through April, but the season there runs through October."

"If you don't have a boat, go to the pier in Gulf Shores," Spectacklelures Captain Yano Serra said. "Go anywhere there's a pier. Mullet point at Fort Morgan is good, but you have to be careful because a fast-moving tide can wash you out."

The Gulf State Park Pier, Alabama Department of Conservation and Natural Resources' Marine Resources Division Chief Marine Biologist Kevin Anson said, is drawing even more fish now than it has in the past.

"This pier was made to be the largest pier in the Gulf, though the pier in Navarre is adding some structure. I guess they're beginning to have a pier war," Anson laughed.

"The pier now is significantly longer than the last pier before (Hurricane) Ivan destroyed it, and it reaches a little deeper water, and people are actually catching more reef fish there now, which is kind of an oddity. The state deposited some artificial fishing reefs to enhance the habitat around the pier when it was constructed in 2009. That was done to try to do what reefs do, provide habitat for fish."

Perdido Pass is a heavily fished area, but it contains some of the best structural features on the beach. Both sides of the pass are reinforced with jetties, large rocks to protect the shore from erosion, and the west side of the pass has a long seawall that's highly productive when the water's moving in or out. On the west side you can also have a lot of luck fishing near the bridge pilings from the seawall.

No matter where you go, talk to other anglers about what's biting, guides say. "If you're fishing somewhere, around Perdido Pass, for example, and you see people fishing there, watch and learn and get some tips from those people fishing there. Ask what bait they're using," Captain Childress said.

Good advice.

Gotta Go!
Are the places mentioned in this section the only places you can catch fish? Not at all. Should you make a special trip to fish them? Maybe. Should they be the only places you try your hand at fishing? Never! Fish where the fish are biting, and use the techniques you find here to identify those places!

66

VI. Putting It All Together

Whacha think, Matt? Think we ought to go fishing tonight?" I'd fished with Granddaddy for years at that point, but it was the first time he'd ever asked my opinion on whether it'd be worth it to put the boat in and go floundering.

Now, floundering has a lot of variables, so I thought about it for a minute before I replied.

"That moon's gone down. Shouldn't be too bright," I began.

"Yep. But do you think the water'll be clear enough?"

"Well, we got rain last week, but it should be clear by now."

"Yep." I began to get some more confidence.

"And the wind's not too bad. It ought to be pretty calm."

"Yeah, you're right."

"And it's out of the west today," I said, looking around quickly to make sure I was right.

"Well, I'll call Johnny."

Johnny Oblak was short, slight but

strong and surefooted as a cat. When we'd crank up the outboard and plane out as we crossed over to the Pirate's Cove side at Orange Beach he'd squat on the bow of the boat with one hand on the striped painter's hat he always wore and the other rested on his knee. I always thought he'd fall head over heels into the boat if we hit a big wave. I could just see him soaring off the front of the boat if we struck a log floating in that pitch-black darkness where water and shore and sky all merge into one lightless void, but he never did.

I was pretty proud of myself for giving the right answers, and I sipped coffee sitting between Granddaddy and Johnny Oblak on the way to the boat launch, warmed further by the idea that I'd gotten to be a pretty wise guy. Johnny must've sensed it.

"Oh, boy. We sure messed up tonight."

"Oh, boy. We sure messed up tonight," he said as we eased up the Intercoastal Canal bridge. My ears itched, and my head shot around.

"What do you mean, Mr. Johnny?" I asked cautiously, looking out the window where he looked down toward the canal, frowning at the growing shadows in the last moments before full darkness took hold.

"Well, we ain't gonna be able to see a thing," he said.

"What? That water's got to be clear," I said. "It hasn't rained in more than a week!"

"Well, I don't think we'll be able to see a thing," Johnny said as

Granddaddy pulled the knob to turn on the old Ford's headlights. "Just look down there at the water. You can see it from here. It's pitch black! We won't be able to see nothing!"

Oh, they had a nice laugh. Shaking my head, I realized I could still learn a thing or two from these two old goats.

"You look there, Matt," Johnny said later that night as we drank coffee in the dark. "You see that shoreline? Mark that in your mind. Remember that. What it looks like. Remember how many lights you see there, and the treeline, everything about it.

"One day, Matt, you'll come down here to flounder and you won't see any of it. It'll all be gone. They'll put up buildings and condos and it won't look anything like it does now. You won't recognize it."

Johnny was right. I sure miss him. There's still a lot I could learn.

Fighting a Fish

Fish On! So you've got your seven-foot, medium-action rod, your spinning reel with 200-300 yards of 12-pound monofilament, tackle to tie Carolina rigs and good, fresh bait. You've spotted a likely piece of structure, and you've got your bait hooked and waiting for a bite in some moving water.

Congratulations, you've put it all together.

The only question now is what you'll do when that monster hits the line. The unpredictability of saltwater fishing means that you might get just about anything on the other end, so it's worth taking some time to get some tips about what to do with it when it's hooked.

"The main thing I tell people is to keep the rod up and let the drag do the work, the drag and the rod," Bay Ranger Captain Frank Ford said. "Take your time; take it slow and easy. I preach that. Just about everybody wants to crank it through the rod tip. Take your time and enjoy the fight. It takes a lot of time to get the fish on the line. Take some time to land it."

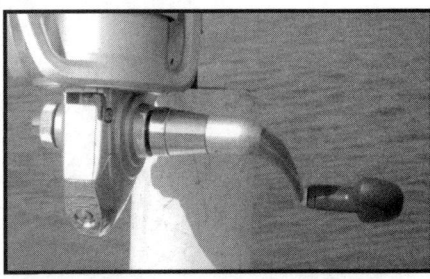

Most spinning reels are designed to allow you to mount the crank lever on either side of the reel. Which side should you use? It's considered best for a right-handed angler to use the left-hand option to mount the crank lever so that the right hand can hold the rod and feel the fish. If you feel more comfortable reeling with your dominant hand, however, there's no law against that.

Fishing salt water can mean catching bigger fish than you might be experienced at fighting. The experts say to keep your drag set on the light side.

"I only want two or three pounds of pressure on the drag," Ford said. "You just want to be able to grab the line with your hand and pull it out relatively easily. If it's too light and you catch a small fish and it's peeling the drag off, you'll realize it's too light and you can tighten it up a little bit, but if it's too tight you'll get broken off."

Back Bay Captain Don Holloway tells his clients to be careful of making a mistake that can allow the fish to get off the line.

"Keep pressure on the line," he said. "Never let the line go slack, and don't

Don't Fight the Feeling!
Rods made with modern materials are designed to deliver information to you, the angler, through your hands. When you feel the fish fighting harder or softening its resistance, act accordingly.

pump the rod. When you do that, if you watch the rod tip, you'll see that when the rod is up the rod tip is bent, and there's tension on the line. When you take it down, it straightens out, and the tension's off the line. That's when a fighting fish will throw the hook. Keep a constant, steady, even pressure as you reel him in. If the fish pulls the line, stop reeling, and when it stops, then reel. That's why the drag is audible. When you hear that, stop reeling, and when it stops, start reeling again."

Captain Ted Childress of Childress Charters warns against causing yourself problems by continuing to reel when a fish is taking line and the drag is engaged.

"If you're using a spinning reel, after you've caught a few nice fish that have taken drag, reeling while they're taking drag is why the line gets tangled up,"

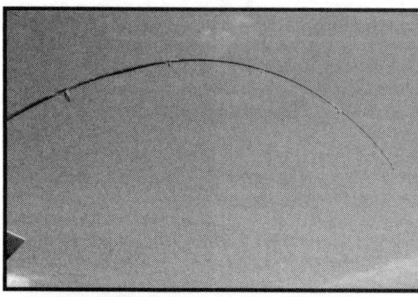

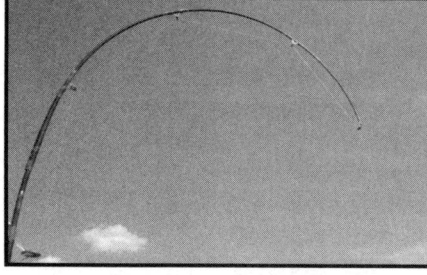

Rods are designed to put the maximum amount of pressure on a fish when bent in a particular way, pictured at top. Avoid doubling the rod over on itself, as the rod in the bottom picture is. Bending a rod in this way risks breaking the rod.

Childress said. "When you're fighting a fish with a spinning reel, and it's taking drag, if you reel while it's taking drag, it's twisting the line up. You have to let the fish take the drag. Most people want to reel and reel and reel, just sit there and reel as fast as they can. You have to stop reeling and let the fish take the line on the drag. Use the rod to your advantage. The rod does a lot more work than you think."

Captain DeJuan Tedder of Gulf Adventures makes the point that the reel doesn't fight the fish, the rod does. "If he's pulling the line, let him take it. When he stops, then reel," Tedder said. "You'll break the fish's spirit. He'll get tired. The more pressure you keep on a fish, the quicker you'll wear him out. The reel's just there to get the line back; the rod's what you catch him with."

"Don't rush the fish. Always play the fish down so it's not green when you try to get it to the beach."

The Audrey II's David Brown cautions about impatience. "Don't rush the fish. Always play the fish down so it's not green when you try to get it to the beach," he said. Once you get it there, Captain Jeff Chambliss said, use every advantage you can to land the fish.

"Have patience. Don't set the drag too tight to begin with. If it takes drag, let him have it. That's what it's for," Chambliss said. "When you get him close, move him in the right direction, and then swiftly move him in on the beach. Bring him in with a wave if you can. Let the fish wear himself out."

Want some more tips? Here are some things that can make your day run a lot smoother.

Tips From The Pros

On preparation:

Be prepared. Have a few leaders made up ahead of time so you don't have to stop and cut and tie them. If you have some made up and the fish are biting it could save you. You've got to get the line back in the water while they're there. Those fish move up and down the beach."

— Captain Jeff Chambliss

On toothy critters:

The main difference between fresh water and salt water? Teeth! If you're fishing with high-dollar lures you might want to use at least a 20-pound monofilament leader or something even heavier if you're fishing around the jetties, 30-pound at the minimum, or wire because of the teeth on fish like bluefish or Spanish Mackerel."

— Captain Jeff Chambliss

On really toothy critters:

Be mindful of sharks if you're fishing on the surf. Think. Do you really want to walk out to where it's chest deep? If I was on the beach and I saw a lot of birds working I wouldn't want to go down there in the middle of that. I don't mind wading into the water, but it depends on visibility. If

I can see the bottom several yards off I feel a lot better than I would walking in murky water. We do have sharks here that can be dangerous. A bull shark five feet long wouldn't take very long to change your life. If you're in the water where the fish are feeding, the sharks are going to be attracted to the same things you are. I wouldn't want to be chest-deep in an active feeding area. If you see something like that going on in the water around you, get out."

— Captain David Brown

On crabbing:

Don't keep crabs with orange sacks on them. Those are females, and if you keep the females you'll kill all the crabs."

— Captain David Brown

On painful stickers:

Most people don't realize just how bad a salt water catfish sting is. Hot water breaks down the poison, and that works for stingrays, too."

— Captain Jeff Chambliss

On boating:

What people don't understand about boating etiquette is that when you're driving a boat it's either slow or fast. There's no

74

in-between. A boat can draw a huge wake. Either go slow or plane your boat off. You need to look behind the boat and look at how big of a wake you're throwing. You see people in big boats looking like Rodney Dangerfield. Morons. You're also responsible for your wake, and you could have to pay damages."

— Captain Ted Childress

On chartering:

I've got a lot of tips, but the best one is that when you're new to an area and know nothing about that area, the best thing for you to do is do your homework and look up a reputable charter fishing outfit and hire them to take you fishing for the first time. If you really want to learn they're going to teach you different ways to hook stuff up, different ways to fish and different bait to use. You'll see how they catch bait, and you'll get a plethora of knowledge that would take you years to gain. Charter a boat for four hours. It costs you something, but you'll get a ton of knowledge."

— Captain Ted Childress

On doing it yourself:

Rod holders? You can buy those, or you can buy PVC really cheap and make two or three rod holders for next to nothing. It gets your line standing up a little higher.

The key about them is making them a little taller. The higher up you get them the less the line is affected by the waves. The lower they are to the water the more the breakers at shore catch the line. I always make mine tall, almost to shoulder height. That way the line's way above the breakers."
— Captain Bobby Abruscato

VII. The Payoff

I'd woken up on the floor in the den, and it'd taken me a minute to get my bearings. Sleeping in a bed wasn't allowed when you smelled like flounder.

Outside, Granddaddy was cleaning fish. His hands moved the blade over each fish in turn. First, he'd scrape off the scales. Then he'd make a cut on the belly and use the tip of the filet knife to scrape out the guts. Then he'd move the knife down the flounder's spine all the way to the tail, flip the filet over, cut it the filet free, flip over the fish and cut off the other filet. It all moved so fast I could barely see the knife-blade move. He'd grab the water hose and spray off the guts into a five-gallon bucket and reach into the ice chest without looking for the next fish.

Occasionally he'd stop for a moment and look at one, gauging its thickness and admiring our catch. Later that night we'd have home fries and hushpuppies and usually some pie or cake when we were done. I can't remember the freezer ever not having fish.

When he was done he'd wash off the board. For a week or so you'd still see the scales next to the driveway when you walked by. One thing I learned for sure in those days: Fishing can work up an appetite, but if you do it right you'll never be hungry.

The Catch

Y ou'll probably catch a lot of white trout, some ground mullet or whiting, and you could catch anything from a ladyfish to a bluefish to a Spanish Mackerel, a pompano or a flounder. Redfish are out there off the shore, and black drum and even small sharks," A-Team Fishing's Captain Bobby Abruscato said.

Redfish, one of the most common species of gamefish caught in this area, are easily identified by the spot, or spots, on their tails.

In the Gulf waters near the shore, the possibilities for catches are almost limitless.

"You can catch a lot of fish from right in front of the condo off the beach," Childress Charters' Captain Ted Childress said. "You'll have a chance of catching speckled trout, Spanish Mackerel, redfish, bluefish, pompano or skipjack (ladyfish)."

The variety and sheer numbers of fish available right off the shore is one of the draws that brings people to the Gulf

78

Shores and Orange Beach area year after year.

Alabama Department of Conservation and Natural Resources' Marine Resources Division Chief Marine Biologist Kevin Anson keeps tabs on what's caught year-round.

"We have, primarily, from the traditional beach or bank-fishing standpoint, those individuals catching

Piles of rocks designed to halt erosion are known as jetties, and they create a habitat preferred by gamefish like sheepshead.

anything from red drum (redfish) to spotted sea trout in spring and early summer to what locals call whiting, what we scientists call kingfish," Anson said. "Gulf kingfish and the southern kingfish are the more commonly caught of the three, and there's also a northern kingfish, but it's very rare in our waters."

Childress said the time of year can affect what you'll catch from the shore. "In March through April you'll start to see the sheepshead fire up. The pompano will fire up, and you're going to catch a lot of those off the beach. Sheepshead like to hang around the rocks and the jetties. In the wintertime fishing off the beach you'll catch whiting, which are kind of like ground mullet and have good white meat."

Anson echoed Childress' words about the seasonality of fishing on the coast. "I'd stress that there's a marked difference in the availability of fish from season to season. There's a dramatic shift in the number and the species available in spring, summer and early fall. A lot of fish have some migration patterns or they're simply in shallow water in the summer when it's warmer."

Bay Ranger Captain Frank Ford said not knowing what you'll catch is half the fun. "You can be fishing for trout and catch a ten-pound redfish," he said. "Bigger than that sometimes. You may tangle into a shark or a Jack Cravalle, a grouper, or snapper or almost anything. It's available, and that's the lure to saltwater fishing, not knowing what you'll catch. If you have a bait in the water, you can catch any number of different species."

"(Fishermen might catch) Spanish Mackerel, though that's more from a pier-fishing standpoint than purely beach or bank-fishing," Anson said. "Nonetheless, they're caught from the shore, as well as bluefish, and flounder is also available, that's Southern and Gulf flounder, and also from the pier, King Mackerel, cobia, which are also called ling and lemon fish, though ling is the common name locals use, and there's ladyfish, which are a non-food fish."

Where you fish could affect what you end up with in your cooler, too, Chambliss Charters' Captain Ted Chambliss said. "If you're fishing from the beach you'll probably catch a lot of catfish, some whiting and hopefully some pompano. You might catch redfish," he said. "Your chances go way

Length:
Tail Length and Fork Length are two different things in the eyes of the law. Make sure when you determine whether a fish is a keeper or one to be released that you apply the proper measurement method.

up if you fish from the pier. Flounder are a good bet, Spanish Mackerel, bluefish, hardtails, ladyfish; they're all possibilities."

"We have a quite a few fish that are caught and targeted and preferred by shore anglers, and the majority are caught in spring, summer or early fall, though weather affects these things," Anson said. "We can still have a fishery for pompano, depending on the weather, in the winter, and even see Spanish mackerel being caught a little early."

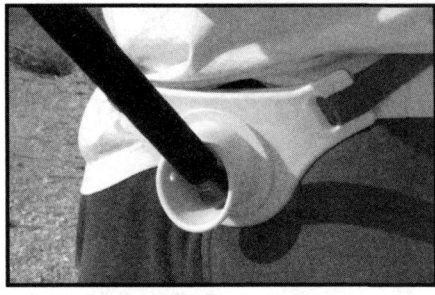

A fighting harness may not be a bad idea even when fishing from the shore in salt water. It's not uncommon to fight a fish for an extended period of time, especially on lighter tackle.

Beyond those fish, barracuda, King Mackerel and sharks, including black-tip and hammerhead, are all possible catches. Get a tide chart from a local bait or tackle store for more details about identifying your catch, creel limits for a particular species and size limits. Anson said creel limits and size restrictions are laws that are for the good of the fishery. "It is a public resource, and as such it's been deemed renewable, and so that it's here for the next generation and beyond conservation should be one of the guiding principals for anyone fishing.

"Bag or creel limits are imposed where fishing pressure could exceed the biological capacity of the fish to reproduce," Anson explains. "We need to have enough fish in the population to continue the species." Size limits, he said, are guided by the same principals.

"Some fish may have minimum size limits that are much larger than other fish, and likewise, lower bag limits. It depends on how often that fish reproduces and what the reproductive strategy is for that fish, whether it's a nest builder, for example, or casts its eggs off in the water column. It also depends on the survival rate of the fish," Anson said.

How Big is BIG?

Finally, you might wonder about the size of the fish you'll be catching off the shore.

"The bigger ones of those we've mentioned are the black drum and the red drum in the 20-pound range," Anson said. "Reds can get up to 25 pounds, and you'll catch the occasional 30-pound fish. Black drum can get up to 50 or 60 pounds. For those folk fishing from shore or even in inland waters like the Intercoastal Canal, they'll get 30- or 40-pound black drum in the springtime when they're running."

"Reds can get up to 25 pounds, and you'll catch the occasional 30-pound fish."

In salt water, big is really big. "King mackerel will get up to 30 pounds," Anson said, "And cobia will get up to 40 or 50 pounds if it's a good year for them."

Handling Your Catch

Once you catch your fish, be aware of what to do with them.

If you're planning on eating your catch, you must put the fish on ice as soon as you can, preferably as soon as you land it and clear the hook. Keep a cooler for your catch, and keep your catch separate from bait and snacks. For best results, gut your fish as soon as possible and keep fresh fish on ice at all times.

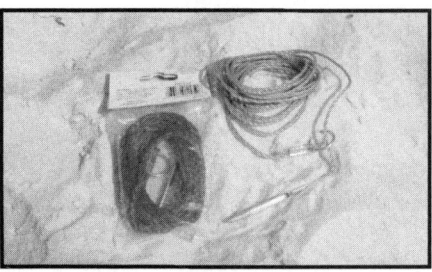

Stringers come in different styles, but any stringer should be used by attaching the fish through the bottom jaw instead of stringing the line through the fish's gills.

The Alabama Department of Public Health offers some guidelines on safe fish handling in its publication, "Get Hooked on Health:"

• Keep fish cold until ready to cook. Fish must be kept on ice or in the refrigerator to prevent spoiling.

• Store fish in the refrigerator within two hours after cooking or serving.

• Eat only thoroughly cooked fish. Uncooked fish may contain viruses and parasites that can make you sick.

• Eat only the fillet portions of fish. Contaminants that may come from the environment can accumulate in fatty tissues, especially when fish are large. Remove and discard the skin, guts, and liver. Filleting removes fat that is located in the belly flaps and along the lateral line of the back.

Fish On! Shore: Gulf Shores/Orange Beach

If you use a stringer, make sure to anchor it securely. A stringer will keep fish alive and fresh until you're ready to clean them. It's better to pierce the fish's lower jaw though the fleshy part near the tip than to string it through a gill.

Cleaning fish should be done in sanitary conditions. Make sure you have a source of fresh water handy to rinse frequently, and don't forget to rinse your hands. Fillet knives are very sharp, and you'll want to keep a good grip on them. Fillet gloves to protect against cuts are available at bait and tackle shops locally and aren't a bad idea.

To clean most fish, begin by scaling the fish. Next, make a cut down the fish's belly beginning under its gills, and remove the guts. Make a triangular cut to remove its vent, or anal opening, on its underside near the tail. If the fish is too small to fillet, simply cut off the head by making cuts on both sides beginning behind the gills and angled slightly toward the front of the fish.

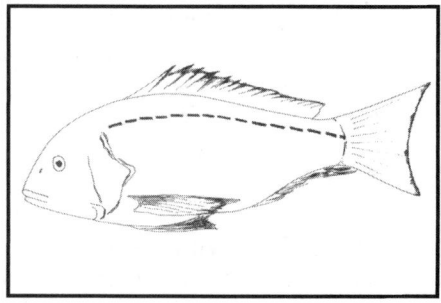

Most fish are cleaned similarly. Note where cuts are properly made to produce filets.

Remember to consult state law before cleaning fish at your fishing location, as it may be illegal to do so before going home.

To fillet a fish, begin by making a cut behind the gills downward toward the fish's midsection. Stop when you encounter the rib bones. Make a cut down the length of the fish along one side of its spine, and peel the fillet downward. Continue to deepen the cut, removing the meat on the fish's side. Turn the fish over and repeat the process on the other side. If the fillet is large enough, cut it into pieces by slicing it from top to bottom.

Make sure to clean fish meat thoroughly, and keep it on ice until you're ready to cook it. If you plan to transport fish meat a long distance, make provisions to keep it on ice until you reach your destination. Never eat fish that hasn't been properly handled.

Catching and Releasing

If you don't plan on eating your catch, or if you're not allowed to keep your catch by state law, releasing the fish isn't just responsible, it's your duty.

Fish can live for a short period of time out of water, but it's best to return them to the water as quickly as possible. You've got time for a quick picture, but be mindful that you're stressing the fish, and always treat the fish with the respect it deserves.

Sportfishing
Some fish like gafftopsail cats have little value as food. These fish should always be caught and released. Remember, part of being a responsible angler includes stressing a fish as little as possible in case you have to release it.

To properly release a fish, first remove the hook from its mouth using a hook removal device or a pair of needle-nosed pliers. Be careful to cause as little damage as possible. When handling the fish, be aware that damaging its skin or scales can cause infections, and avoid rubbing off any protective slime you might encounter on the fish's skin.

In most cases, it's best to handle a fish

at the mouth, though with sharp-teethed fish this isn't advisable. When that's the case, hold the fish by it's gill-plate, but be careful to avoid damaging its gill membranes.

In many cases, the landing process can be exhausting to a fish. When returning it to the water, cradle it by the belly or hold it lightly by the tail in the water, allowing water to pass through the fish's mouth and past its gills. This should revive the fish, and it will swim away on its own power when it's ready.

VIII. At The End of The Day

Granddaddy was a quiet person, owning, I always thought, to his being hard of hearing. After he got a good hearing aid, though, he still kept his mouth shut most of the time.

We'd put the boat in and worked around some piers after dark, and we hadn't seen a single flounder yet. It was my first time gigging, and I'd held the long pole at the ready for what seemed like an eternity. The night was dark and warm, and my 12-year-old legs were tiring from standing there behind Granddaddy as he poled smoothly along in about three feet of water.

He'd showed me a print, the faint outline of an oval-shaped flounder where the fish had laid for a while and left. He'd explained to me how they settled down on the bottom and buried themselves, how both of their eyes were on their top side, and how they'd ambush unsuspecting bait fish. It was all new and amazing to me, and I did my best to soak up the knowledge, repeating it to myself in the quiet dark when he'd quit talking.

We'd taken a break and crossed over to the Pirate's Cove side, a long, flat, featureless bottom where no piers jutted out into the water and no structures broke the short pine treeline on the shore. I focused on the bottom, ignoring needlefish that swam along with us on the edge of the light from the 40-watt bulbs on the bow. I peered intently at every footprint left by the long-legged birds that picked through the shallows hunting for small fish. I felt my heart quicken, then fall as a stick casting a long shadow came into view, then disappeared. Once I even put the gig down on the shape of a flounder, feeling the gig head sink into sand.

"Just a print." My eyes had begun playing tricks on me. Could be I was tired, as staying up all night was pretty uncommon for me at that age.

"Just a print," Granddaddy said.

My eyes had begun playing tricks on me. Could be I was tired, as staying up all night was pretty uncommon for me at that age. Finally, after long thought and consideration, I came out and asked the question I hadn't been able to find a good answer for.

"Granddaddy, how do you know? I mean, how do you know it's a flounder?"

"You'll know," he said.

You'll know.

Now You Know

There's something about fishing that sets those who do it, those who love it, apart.

Maybe it's the knowledge of water and fish habits and weather and tackle and how to combine it all to achieve an end, a fish in your hands. Maybe this book has given you some of that knowledge, a foundation to build on. I hope so.

Maybe it's the confidence, the pride that comes from pitting yourself against nature, against the sea itself, against creatures worthy and noble, and prevailing, coming out on top, winning. I hope you'll feel that soon, too.

Maybe it's inclusion, the sense of belonging, when you talk to others involved in the same effort, the same unyielding pursuit. If you can experience that anywhere, it's here, on the shore of this beautiful Gulf God's given us.

Maybe it's those things, but I think it's this: I think it's what Granddaddy taught me that night floundering, that first night I spent gigging.

You'll know.

Fish for a while, and you'll begin to sense things about the world around you, the water in front of you, the sand under your feet. You'll begin to feel the pull of the waves, the way the sea shapes the shore, the way the sun's movement in the sky affects you as much as it affects the fish. You'll find yourself joined, in some small way, to creation in a way you may have never felt before, joined not as visitor, but as participant, as brother, as sister.

You'll know. Whether it's time to change your bait. Whether it's best to move down the beach a little. Whether it's a good idea to take a break for a bit and just watch the birds running along the sand. Whether it's better to cast a little closer, or a little farther out or to just leave your line alone for a spell. You'll know. You'll begin to trust yourself, your instinct, your heart.

You'll know. When your buddy needs a hook. When a passer-by needs a smile. When a child needs a hug and an "atta-boy." When the fisherman down the beach needs some bait. You'll know. That's what sets an angler apart, that's what I hope you'll take from this book, and that's why you wanted to do this in the first place.

How will you know?
You'll know.

You'll know.

Equipment Checklist

So you're ready to outfit up; here's what you'll need. The items listed first are the bare necessities. Listed beneath those are some items that can make your day fishing more enjoyable and easier. If you want to catch some fish from the shore, here's what you'll need to have.

Rod, 7-foot, Medium action
Reel, Spinning (200-300 yard of 12-pound-test capacity)
300 yards of 12-pound-test monofilament line
50 yards of 20-pound-test leader line (mono)
12-24 barrel swivels (two-eye, dark-colored)
6-12 egg weights (3/8-oz.)
6-12 egg weights (1/2-oz.)
6-12 egg weights (1-oz.)
6-12 pyramid weights (1-oz.)
12-24 No. 2 hooks (J or circle, dark-colored)
Landing net
Bait (shrimp, live or fresh)
Flow-troll bucket or aerator (if you're using live bait)
Sunscreen (30 SPF minimum; sunburn is no joke)
Bait knife
Hook removal device (needle-nose pliers work fine)
Tide calendar with creel/size limits

If you're on a budget, the items listed above will be enough to get you fishing the right way, and you can get them all for a reasonable cost. If you've got a little more to spend, consider getting the following; they could make your day a lot easier.

Sand spike (rod holder)
Beach/camp chair
A variety of hook styles (circle, treble, small circle hooks for sheepshead)
Fillet knife

If you're looking for a long-term outfit, grab the items listed above, and take a look at the following items in the bait and tackle store.

Live bait bucket (for use with aerator)
Fishing gloves
Sand flea scoop
Sabiki rig
Cast Net
50 yards fluorocarbon leader line
Steel leaders

Inshore Guides

The inshore guides featured in this book are some of the top experts on the coast when it comes to fishing. As one guide said, the best way to learn fishing in this water is to get a guide to take you out and show you how it's done.

Whether you've fished before or become an old salt at fishing these waters, a day with an inshore guide is a memory you'll hold for a lifetime. On a personal level, I couldn't have written this book without them, and I can promise they're some of the nicest and most knowlegable folk you'll ever come across.

Give one a call today.

Capt. Bobby Abruscato
A-Team Fishing Adventures
(251) 661-7696

www.ateamfishing.com
bobbyabruscato@yahoo.com

Captain David Brown
1-4 passengers
(251) 981-6246 or (251) 942-4037
Light tackle, inshore trips, 4-6 hours
Day or night, fly fishing

brownsinshore@yahoo.com
www.brownsinshore.com

Captain DeJuan Tedder
No Excuses
Gulf Adventures
1- 6 passengers
(251) 978-9711
Inshore and nearshore charter
fishing

gulfadventures@yahoo.com
www.gulfadventures.net

Captain Don Holloway
Back Bay
4 passengers
(251) 550-5418
Inshore guide services, day & night

captholloway@yahoo.com

Captain Jeff Chambliss
Baby Therapy
1-4 passengers
(251) 981-2463 or (251) 979-1209
Inshore fishing, trout, redfish,
flounder

chambliss@gulftel.com

Captain Frank Ford
Bay Ranger
Up to six passengers
(251) 981-4796
Inshore, nearshore, back bay, day
and night

starfish@gulftel.com
www.myislandtimecharters.com

Captain Ted Childress
Childress Charters
1-6 passengers
(251) 458-5873
Inshore fishing, speckle trout, redfish,
pompano, sheephead, flounder, etc.
and sightseeing

childresscharters@gmail.com

Captain Yano Serra
Speck-Tackle-Lure
Inshore fishing charters, specialized
guide services for fly fishing redfish,
speckle trout, etc.
Dauphin Island, Alabama

24-foot Nautiqe Star, 250 Yamaha
Inshore bull reds, speckle trout,
flounder and slot reds
(251) 610-0462

www.specktacklelure.com
captainyano@hotmail.com

94

Thanks

I'd be remiss if I didn't make mention of some folk without whom this book would never have been what it is. To them, and all those whom I've forgotten (and I can't imagine there aren't some): I owe you.

My illustrator (and my cousin) Alesia Horn Aaron, caught the gist of my harried requests like an absolute pro. If anyone can tie a Uni knot after reading this, it's all her doing.

Gary Heidelberg did a phenomenal job at reviewing the content in this book. He put his engineer's eye on the details and made some suggestions that unquestionably enriched it, and his encouragement got me fired up. In additon to being a world-class angler, Gary's also my uncle; do I have a great family or what!

Jared Barker has been my sounding board on business, backwoodsery and big country western fishin'. When I needed to get the feeling for fishing as I wrote, edited and laid this book out, I called him.

Lucia Partin was the first person to tell me I could write, and she took me under her wing when I started teaching. Thanks, Lucia.

Finally, to Dana, Peco, the writers in my circle and everyone else whose encouragement kept me going, heartfelt thanks and love.

I know, it's gettin' sappy. Sue me; it's my first book.

Love,
— Matt

Contact Clay House
on the Web!

For news, information, to order copies of this and other great titles, or to send comments and pictures of big fish, visit:

www.clayhousebooks.com

Like us on FaceBook!
We want to know what you think!
http://www.facebook.com/ClayHousePublishing

Fishin' notes: